THE WAYS OF LOVE

BIOGRAPHY

Camilla G. Iannacci attended Lectures, Seminars on Philosophy at 'S. Carlo Foundation' in Modena, at the Departments of Philosophy of the Universities of Turin and Florence.

She collaborated with Giacinto Plescia:

- Graduated in Architecture at the Polytechnic University of Turin
- Former Project Researcher and Temporary Contractor at CNR
- Participated some Calls EU and CNR.

She received:

- the Cdcalendarspirelliinternetional for the Essay 'About Time' 1997;
- the 1st Prize of the 'Pegaso-Dire' Poetry Competition in Biella;
- the 2nd Prize of Poetry 'The Piazzetta' in Salerno
- the 2nd Prize of the Prose Competition 'Pegasus' in Biella;
- She ranked third in the Literary Prize 'La Pira' in Pistoia.

- Some of her Poems are online: www.espresso.it;
- some stories on: 'La Repubblica-Firenze'.

She has been reviewed in:

- "Storie", Feltrinelli – MI
- "History of Italian Literature" - Helicon Ed. by Prof. N. Bonifazi, Foreword by Prof. G. Luti
- She participated in:
- the 8th Poetry Prize 'W. Tobagi' in Ateneo Veneto
- the 'M. Luzi' Prize;
- the 'Focus' Prize.
- the CNR Call Promotion Research-Typology "Publication Paper: Historical, Philosophical and Italian Literary with particular attention to Contemporary Reflection" with the Research 'The Principle of Indeterminacy as Hermeneutics of the Relationship between man and Physis'

Publications:

- A Simple Friendship with Rossana Rossanda, a short Correspondence;
- Ferragni and Fedez: Analysis and Morpho-genesis of a Singularity in the Info-Space-Time of Social Media;
- Ferragni and Fedez: Media-Morphosis. Aphorism

about the Ferragnez

- Desideranza
- Philopoiesis

Bibliography:

- Giacinto Plescia: Ontology of the Physis
- Giacinto Plescia: Epistemic, Nothingness and Art
- Giacinto Plescia: Ontology of Physis: Hermeneutics and Epistemics of Mathematical Physics, Godel-Heidegger-Thom
- Giacinto Plescia: Ontology of Art, Ontological Epistemic
- Giacinto Plescia: Kalipso's song, the Goddess of the Sublime, the Nothing and the Sublime, a New Ontology of the Work of Art
- Giacinto Plescia: Ontology of the Myth
- Giacinto Plescia: Ontology of the Sublime
- Giacinto Plescia: Ontology of the Work of Art: the Beauty between Nodes, Ribbons and Singularity, for a Morphogenesis and Topology of Art
- Giacinto Plescia: A Topological Model of Mind the Problem of Consciousness
- Giacinto Plescia: Epistemic and Art: the Beauty after the Nothint
- Giacinto Plescia: Onthodynamis

- Giacinto Plescia: The Chaosmos: is Infinite, Infinitesimal
- Giacinto Plescia: Ontology of Mathesis and the Crisis of Foundations
- Giacinto Plescia: Hi-Tech Spatiality: Technocities, Highways, Valleys
- Giacinto Plescia: Analysis of Post-industrial Spatial-Archemorphism
- Giacinto Plescia: Space Archeomorphs of Innovance: Technology, Production and Media

Summary

INTRODUCTION

"Lovers are in a hurry to say #TiAmo and anticipate every move and decision that prevents them from saying #TiAmo anytime, anywhere and anytime: they wouldn't be in love differently. Love has its reasons: it is a truth that does not admit or know objections. But "how to return to the truth of love in the epoch of its end?": We return to the truth only from the roots: thinking about #TiAmo: the simplest and "philosophical" verb of all: #TiAmo ": I know, you think so. Saying #TiAmo is worth challenging the Tractatus logico-philosophicus Wittgenstein for which "on what we cannot talk about, we must be silent" and talk and it is immediately evident that it does not know reasonableness, only excess loves #TiAmo : it is absolute and pre-powerful like a child alone between the unspeakable and the undecidable there is the #TiAmo. And "what do I think when I don't think about you? What does not-thinking about you mean? " : When I think "I don't think about you": 1st I think, 2 ^ I am looking for the epochè from #TiAmo, 3 ^ I don't go out, 4 ^ I think I don't think about you in thinking about you, 5 ^ the "I don't think of you" or the "I think of you linked to #TiAmo, is other than" I think "and, even if it finds a root in it, it distances itself from it: it inhabits a territory whose borders are not dominated .

Perhaps the "discourse" on love is a return to "mania" and mythos because it cannot be objectified, it is not clear and distinct: it experiences the abyss, the undecidable and precisely when and if it tries to say itself it discovers its limits and it can only be an autobiography, a story, a poem, a work of art, a singularity that speaks to other singularities. The #TiAmo is followed by "forever,": which is not always forever but to live it cannot be separated from it and above all the #TiAmo is intertwined with "madness": in fact we say "I love you madly": philosophy can speak, groped a discourse on incandescence, on the passion suffered - therefore - by the ego which - therefore - is dispossessed of it.

CHAPTER ONE
Definitions Of Love That Everyone Should Know

Love is said to be pure, painful, sweet, and dreadful, all at the same time. Love is, in reality, a simple need in everyone's life. To live a proper and safe life, everyone requires love. Love can be described in a variety of ways. If you ask anyone what love is to them, they will give you their own meaning. Love encompasses a wide range of thoughts, feelings, and attitudes. For certain people, love is more than just a sexual attraction; it is also an emotional bond.

Love is more of a feeling that a person has for someone else. People always mix up passion and desire. Being truly devoted and attached to someone or something is what love entails. The fundamental definition of love is to have more than a passing admiration for another. It is a relationship between two parties.

Love Doesn't Hurry Into Relationships

Give yourself and your partner some alone time. Take it easy on yourself. Know what they do and don't like. Consider if you would be able to share a shared bond in the future. Every person has certain behaviours that irritate you.

Consider this: if you saw a person's dark side, would you really feel the same way?

Love Is Not Being Jealous

In situations where true love is present, envy and possessiveness have no place. While it is natural to be defensive in a relationship, there should be a mutual understanding. Being too invested in a relationship will cause the other person to feel suffocated. They may have an ex-boyfriend with whom they have a friendly relationship, but it didn't work out while they were dating. That is why they have moved on and are now with you.

Love Is Giving Yourself A Chance

It doesn't mean things won't turn out just because you have a disagreement over something. Give yourself a chance to succeed. It's possible that your experience and your partner's perception aren't the same. That is, in some ways, what makes life fun!

Love Is To Stop Expecting

Stop expecting doesn't imply that you've given up on yourself. However, don't ask your mate to do just as you expect them to do. It's not appropriate. Your relationship's expectations of you can vary from what your partner expects of you. Respect the fact that they aren't exactly like you. The longer you want to change others and make them do what you want, the less attached they will get to you.

Love Is Maintaining Privacy

We prefer to address issues over the internet rather than we do in person, with social media freely available to post all your troubles and people willing to leap to your rescue. That is everything you can never do. Maintain the relationship's secrecy. Discuss your concerns with your mate. Don't use social media to air your grievances over something that isn't right for you two. It's important to give your relationship some privacy.

Love Is Avoiding Misunderstandings

When there is a difference of opinion, it is possible to misinterpret. Try to stay away from it. Allow your companion the opportunity to express their point of view. If they're incorrect, speak to them on why you believe they're incorrect. Don't make hasty judgments and add to the drama. This is very harmful to your relationship.

Accepting the other person for who they are is the essence of love. True love is encouraging your mate to pursue their goals while still loving each other. True love is a divine sensation that leaves you feeling complete. It is worthwhile to struggle and put in the effort with one another. Being there with each other through thick and thin is what love is all about. Love is difficult to describe in sentences, but it can be shown by deeds. Love is being someone's pillar of strength, and it can be found in simple acts of love.

Reasons Why Love Is the Best Feeling In The World

Love makes you happy, makes you hopeful, makes you grateful, makes you inspired, and makes your life transform.

1. Love Makes You Feel Invincible

Love gives you the feeling that you can do something. Your outlook on life is more positive and upbeat. You have the confidence to do things you never thought you could.

2. Love Gives You Incredible Inspiration

When you're in love, you feel empowered. It instils in you a can-do spirit that allows you to take on something, anywhere, at any moment. You get motivated while you're in love. Your outlook is upbeat and still hopeful.

3. Love Makes You Feel Good

When you're in love, you're still blissfully happy.

4. Love transforms you into a romantic hopeful.

When you fall in love, you become a romantic. Love gives you confidence that there is someone out there who is just right for you.

5. Love allows you to let go of your fears.

You become fearless when you love somebody. When you're in love, the things you used to be afraid of vanish. You have your own personal cheerleader in your corner, ready to assist you with anything you need. Since you're so happy, you almost feel safe.

6. Love Makes You Be The Best Version of Yourself

You're a better version of yourself when you're in love. You're kind to all and grateful for everything.

7. Love Makes You Rich

You feel wealthy when you are in love. Since you are so fortunate, you are unconcerned with your finances or material possessions. You have a sense of being wealthy in a meaningful way.

8. Love Puts You In A State of Total Confusion

Love perplexes you; it rocks you to your soul and forces you to reconsider your values. Love is a perplexing topic. It's amazing how much you can feel about others. Love fills you with longing, making you miss your significant other in respects you never imagined.

9. Love Makes You Selfless

You can't help but be enraged by love. It makes you want to do something you've never done before. It teaches you to be selfless in ways you didn't realise were possible. You find yourself prioritising your partner's desires above your own.

10. Love Makes You Believe

You get optimistic when you are in love. It gives you hope for a happily ever after. You wonder if you'll ever find your soulmate when you're single. Love teaches you that anything is conceivable, because when it does, it's really awesome.

What It's Really Like To Fall In Love

• Falling in love with someone is the most wonderful, spiritual, and honestly, indescribable experience one may have. It happens all of a sudden and without warning.

• It takes more than "just lust" to fall in love. There's more to it than "chemistry." It requires time, maturity, and acceptance, as well as both of you, but in the most normal way possible.

• Falling in love necessitates a need to bring forth effort. It's realising that this is where you want to be and with whom you want to spend your time, and being able to go to whatever length to keep that passion alive.

• Falling in love entails accepting their quirks and idiosyncrasies when you find them endearing.

• It entails admiring as well as encouraging them. The look of two people falling in love is real, pure, and natural.

• It's going out of the way for the person because you want to, not that you feel obligated to. You want to help the person in whatever way you can.

• Being in love with someone entails not only listening to their passions and desires, but also seeking opportunities to assist them in realising all of their goals.

• It's not just butterflies in your stomach when you fall in love. It's as if you know this guy was made for you. You're well aware that you were missing something when they came along.

• Falling in love means you're no longer dependent on someone else for your satisfaction and self-assurance. It's being content and optimistic, and letting that person contribute to your contentment.

• Falling in love is finding things in common with someone you've never met before. It's about sharing common interests and still accepting one another's differences.

• Falling in love entails losing them but still feeling secure enough to be apart. It's like keeping the best hidden secret all to yourself when you fall in love with someone.

• There are several different types of love out there, all of which are meaningful and moving in their own way. But true love, being in love, is what we all want. It's the storey of a couple who dies within hours of each other when their hearts have been shattered by their separation.

• It's true that falling in love is a choice, but it's not the one you expect. Allowing yourself to not be afraid is a choice. It's the decision to let go of your own barriers. That is the decision we make when we fall in love, and it is the most difficult to make. But if we do, we're in for a once-in-a-lifetime experience.

Scientifically Proven Signs You're in Love

You may be falling in love if you find yourself leaving routine tasks or becoming unusually optimistic...

One of the strangest and most beautiful experiences a person can go through is falling in love. While everyone's experience is unique, there are certain shared thoughts and emotions that can assist people in recognising when it's happening.

You may be exhibiting one of the more apparent symptoms, such as being unable to think of someone or something else, however, that individual or the signs may be more obfuscated.

1. Thinking this one's special

When you're in love, you start to believe your partner is one-of-a-kind. This conviction is accompanied by a lack of romantic passion for someone else. This single-mindedness, according to Fisher and her colleagues, is caused by elevated levels of core dopamine, a brain chemical implicated in concentration and focus.

2. Focusing on the positive

People who are genuinely in love prefer to reflect on their partner's positive attributes while ignoring his or her negative characteristics. They also concentrate on insignificant incidents and things that remind them of their loved one, daydreaming about these priceless mementos. Elevated levels of central dopamine, as well as a surge in central norepinephrine, a chemical linked to heightened memory in the face of new stimuli, are believed to contribute to this concentrated attention.

3. Emotional instability

Falling in love is well known for causing mental and physiological dysfunction. When your relationship faces even the slightest setback, you alternate between exhilaration, euphoria, increased energy, sleeplessness, lack of appetite, shaking, a pounding pulse, and rapid breathing, as well as fear, panic, and feelings of desperation. These mood swings are similar to what opioid addicts do. When in-love people are given pictures of their loved ones, the same brain regions that activate when a heroin abuser takes a dose are activated. According to experts, falling in love is a type of addiction.

4. Intensifying attraction

When you go through adversity with another, it helps to heighten emotional desire. This response may also be due to central dopamine, as evidence suggests that when a reward is postponed, dopamine-producing neurons in the midbrain become more efficient.

5. Intrusive thinking

According to Fisher, people who are in love record spending more than 85 percent of their waking hours thinking about their "love object." Intrusive thought, as this type of obsessive behaviour is known, may be caused by low levels of central serotonin in the brain, a disorder that has historically been linked to obsessive behaviour.

6. Emotional dependency

Possessiveness, jealousy, fear of rejection, and breakup anxiety are also common symptoms of emotional dependence on a romantic relationship. Fisher and her collaborators, for example, studied the minds of people who saw images of a rejected loved one or someone they were still in love with after that person had rejected them. The functional magnetic resonance imaging (fMRI) revealed activity in many brain regions, including forebrain areas such as the cingulate gyrus, which have been linked to cocaine addiction. The researchers reported in the Journal of Neurophysiology in 2010 that "activation of areas involved in cocaine addiction may better understand the obsessive behaviours correlated with rejection in love."

7. Planning a future

They still yearn for a romantic union with their partner, looking for opportunities to strengthen their bond and fantasizing about their future together.

Another authority on dating, Lucy Brown, a neuroscientist at New York's Albert Einstein College of Medicine, claims that our desire to be with another human is similar to our desire for water and other necessities of life.

"When people look at the face of their loved one and think romantic thoughts, functional MRI experiments indicate that primitive neural mechanisms underlying drive, reward perception, and euphoria are present in almost all. This associates romantic love with survival processes, such as those that make us hungry or thirsty "In 2011, Brown told Live Science about his findings. "Romantic love, in my opinion, is an important aspect of the human reproduction policy. It aids in the formation of pair bonds, which aid in our survival. We were created to be drawn to one another and to feel the magic of love."

8. Feelings of empathy

People who are in love have a strong sense of caring for their loved ones, feeling the other person's suffering as their own and able to go to great lengths for them.

9. Aligning interests

When you fall in love, you can find yourself rearranging your everyday priorities and/or changing your wardrobe, mannerisms, behaviours, or beliefs to best conform with those of your partner.

Even then, it's possible that being yourself is the better option: Fisher discovered that people are drawn to their opposites, at least their "brain-chemical" opposites, in another study she presented in 2013 at the "Being Human" meeting. People with so-called testosterone-dominant personalities (highly analytical, aggressive, and emotionally contained), for example, were often attracted to mates with personalities linked to high oestrogen and oxytocin levels, according to her study. These people were introspective, finding purpose and belonging, and empathetic, caring, trusting, and prosocial.

10. Possessive feelings

Sexual lust for one's beloved is common among those who are profoundly in love, but there are also close emotional ties: When a mate is accused of infidelity, the lust for sex is accompanied by possessiveness, a desire for sexual exclusivity, and intense jealousy. This possessiveness is believed to have arisen such that a person in love will force his or her mate to reject any suitors, ensuring that the couple's courtship continues until conception.

The Difference Between Loving Someone and Being in Love with Them

For many people, romantic passion is a major target. You might think of this love as the pinnacle of romantic experiences, if not the pinnacle of life experiences, whether you've been in love before or have yet to fall in love for the first time.

It's thrilling, even exhilarating, to fall in love with someone. However, these feelings may settle into something a little different over time. This love will seem to be mellow or calm. You might say to yourself, "I love them," rather than "I'm in love with them."

This shift does not actually imply that something is wrong with your relationship. Loving somebody more than falling "in love" with them clearly shows how feelings of love change over the course of a relationship, especially one that lasts a long time.

What It's Like To Be In Love

In general, being in love refers to the strong emotions that arise at the beginning of a relationship.

• infatuation

• Happiness

• Excitement and nervousness

• Sexual attraction and lust

Here's an example of how these feelings could manifest.

1. You feel charged and euphoric around them

It might not seem so, but falling in love is a science phenomenon. Hormones play a big role in being in love, and they can supercharge the emotions and make them wildly fluctuate.

Increases of dopamine and norepinephrine trigger sensations of pleasure, giddiness, nervous enthusiasm, and euphoria while you're around the individual you love.

Serotonin deficiency can exacerbate feelings of infatuation. Sex hormones like testosterone and oestrogen, which increase libido and trigger feelings of desire, also play a role.

Other important hormones like oxytocin and vasopressin aid in the cementing of your attraction by fostering loyalty, empathy, and other long-term attachment factors.

2. You can't wait to see them again, even when they've just left

You still feel alone when your mate leaves, even though you've spent the whole day with them. You're curious as to what they're up to and whether they're worried about you. Maybe you've already made arrangements to meet the next day, but you're still worried about how you'll get along before then.

When you're in love, this is a natural occurrence. And just because it's good for you to spend your time apart from each other doesn't mean you love it. You're more definitely experiencing the agonizing ecstasy of falling in love if you can't help worrying of them and though you're separated.

3. Everything feels exciting and new

Being in love will alter your perspective on life. And mundane tasks like walking to the grocery store can be made more pleasurable. You may even see it in a different light. Since their companion loves them, many people in love are more likely to do new ideas or things they previously disliked.

It's never a bad idea to learn new stuff. In reality, being open to new opportunities is a fantastic quality to possess. However, it's natural to be persuaded by a partner's wishes, just make sure you're not under any obligation to do something you don't want to do.

4. You always make time for them

When you're in love with someone, you usually want to spend as much time as possible with them. You probably find yourself rearranging your plans to see your girlfriend, even though you're busy.

This may also include a curiosity to learn more about them by looking at their hobbies. They'll definitely feel the same way about you and want to spend just as much time getting to know your passions while you're in love.

All of this is fairly typical. It's also normal for people in love to "forget" about their friends for a short period of time. Instead of making passion totally consume you, try to continue to spend time with your peers.

5. You don't mind making sacrifices for them

In the early stages of love, you may feel fully committed to your mate, willing to go to any length to help them get through a difficult situation or simply making their life simpler.

Empathy and your increasing affection for them will fuel your ability to be there for them and assist them in every way you can. However, the hormones associated with passion may have an effect on how you make decisions.

Take the time to consider something that would totally uproot or radically alter your life if you were compelled to do so.

After some thought, you may still want to leave your job and move to a new country with your partner. However, be certain that you really want to do it for yourself.

Every form of love will include sacrifices. In reality, couples who work together to meet each other's needs may have a closer relationship. People in love, on the other hand, have a propensity to leap forward and give assistance without hesitation.

6. You have fantastic sex

An intimate relationship does not have to include sex. When it is, though, it may play a significant role in falling in love. The strength of the hormones involved will influence your sex drive, increasing your appetite for your partner and the depth of your sex experience.

When you're first in love, sex will make you get closer to your mate. Good sexual chemistry will make you feel good about sex and make you want to have more of it. It often doesn't hurt to be curious about each other's sexual preferences.

7. You idealize them

When you're in love, it's easy to romanticize your partner's greatest qualities (great listening skills, artistic ability, warm smile) while overlooking the less appealing ones (doesn't respond to messages promptly, flirts with your friends).

When you're in love, it's natural to reflect on the positive aspects of others. However, keep an eye out for red flags or incompatibilities in the relationship.

Consider what your mates have to say if they find anything out. They aren't in love with your mate, but they have a different outlook and are more likely to find problems you overlook.

What It's Like To Love A Partner

Love comes in a variety of shapes and sizes, and it will evolve over time. When you love your partner but don't feel in love with them, your emotions will change in a variety of ways.

1. You're secure in their affection

When you first fall in love, you might want to show not only an idealised version of your partner, but also an idealized version of yourself. You might, for example, strive to look your best at all times. Or maybe you try to mask weaknesses that you think would turn your lover off.

However, as the relationship becomes stronger, you may become more comfortable being yourself. They won't dump you if you forget to take out the garbage or leave dishes in the oven. You agree that you and your partner will still have morning breath.

This isn't to say you don't make an effort to keep this love alive and well. It just means that you've moved to a rational perspective rather than idealised representations of each other.

2. You don't feel the need to hold back your opinions

It's easy to adopt someone's viewpoints as your own when you're in love with them. You may not be fully aware of this at all times.

You might find it easier to publicly express your feelings with a partner you adore and trust. Since love also conveys a sense of safety, you do not feel compelled to conceal your emotions or thoughts in order to keep the relationship safe. You know you should hash things out even though you have a little disagreement.

3. You see (and accept) the good with the less than good

Your mate, like you, is a flawed human being. Of course,

they have positive characteristics that made you fall in love with them. However, they are bound to have certain personality traits or behaviours that you dislike.

Even something that seemed endearing when you first fell in love, like the way they brush their teeth at the kitchen sink, will make you sigh and roll your eyes.

To love another, you must see them completely and embrace all of their flaws, just as they must see and accept all of you. Minor bugs usually don't matter in the long run.

However, if anything bothers you, you'll probably feel better speaking up about it and working to help and support each other as you evolve.

4. Intimacy might require more effort

You actually had sex all the time while you were madly in love with your girlfriend. You'll still have sex as your relationship settles down, but just less often and with less force.

It might feel as though you've missed everything the first time you fall asleep without having sex or spent a night alone. You may also be concerned about the relationship's demise.

But, more often than not, this simply means that life's

pressures have forced you to schedule time with your mate. Although sexual contact can be less frequent, the work you put into communicating intimately will enhance those moments.

5. The relationship takes more work

When you're head over heels in love, it's convenient to owe your relationship your best. The partnership may seem to be progressing well, if not flawlessly, and the two of you seem to agree on everything.

This isn't a long-term solution. To take care of everyday life, you will need to prioritise your relationship less in the future.

When you're both busy or stressed, spending time together can seem less normal and simple. Joy, on the other hand, requires you to keep striving and making an effort to prove you care.

6. You feel deeply connected

Loving anyone may imply a deep sense of bonding and confidence. You're familiar enough with your mate to rattle off their preferences and dislikes, beliefs, and talents without hesitation.

Is One Better Than The Other?

So, you know you love your partner, but you're starting to

wonder if you're really in love with them. That's entirely acceptable. In reality, knowing that your hormones have calmed down may make you feel relieved.

Some people like the rush of falling in love. Others enjoy the closeness and intimacy that comes with long-term love. For this cause, many people strive for long-term partnerships.

What you want out of a relationship can make one seem better than the other, but both may lead to stable relationships.

Since falling out of love, many people demand divorce. However, just because you're no longer in love with your partner doesn't mean you have to abandon them or that your friendship is destined to fail. It just means you'll have to bring in a little more time to get things back on track.

Can You Go Back To Being In Love With Someone?

If you believe your relationship has missed the "spark" that comes with being in love, you can feel depressed or regret. Perhaps you want sex to be more spontaneous, or you want to be happy to see your partner rather than relaxed.

Talking to a relationship counsellor may help you rekindle the feeling of passion, so here are several other suggestions:

1. Have an interest in what they're thinking and doing. Don't hesitate to sign in on a regular basis. Inquire about their day, making sure you pay attention to their reaction.

2. Make quality time together a priority, even intimacy. This could mean leaving a job function early or cancelling your plans to see a movie with a friend.

3. Don't forget the routine repairs. Consider your friendship to be a vehicle that you depend on to get to and from work. Daily oil changes, tyre rotations, and other maintenance are needed to keep it running. Make a deliberate attempt to talk freely and give love to your relationship on a daily basis. There don't have to be big, extravagant shows. A simple kiss to welcome them home will make a big difference.

The bottom line

Your feelings for your partner may become less strong after you've progressed past the early stages of infatuation. You do not feel the same way about their business. You might also love your time apart.

Don't be concerned. This is fairly common, and it does not have to be the end of the world.

Long-term love necessitates commitment. In the very least, if you and your partner put in effort to preserve your relationship, you would most likely have a good partnership.

You would also be able to keep the sensation of being actively in love alive.

CHAPTER TWO

The Stages Of A Relationship Every Couple Goes Through.

A relationship's stages are cyclical, not linear. A relationship's stages are cyclical, not linear. And those who make it to the fifth and final stage of a relationship, Wholehearted Love, will find themselves looping back to a stage not to repeat the process. They will, though, still find their way out.

Stage 1: The Merge

The Merge, also known as the honeymoon period, is the first stage of a partnership. When a couple first gets together, it's always the original, sweeping romance that dominates them, including an all-consuming delight in our partner's presence and insatiable, romantic sex. People in this stage of a relationship sometimes believe they've met their "dream fit," someone who is uncannily close to them and compatible with them. They feel compelled to be together all of the time, and lines are always blurred. The two seem to be merging, or at least seem to be ready to do so.

The logical portion of our brain is often drowned out by these feelings. Indeed, evidence suggests that this first stage is characterized by hormonal modifications in our brain, including a cocktail of hormones like dopamine, oxytocin, and endorphins, which activate and sustain a state of infatuation. This brain glow will make us "addicted" to our partners, causing us to overlook incompatibilities, red flags, and other problems.

What To Do In This Relationship Stage.

Enjoy this stage to the fullest; it's what makes dating so interesting and enjoyable. Be conscious of the heightened feelings at the same time. Take a moment to reflect on your feelings and your friendship, and ask yourself if this person is really the right fit for you. When under the influence of this biochemical love potion, seek candid suggestions from friends to ensure you're not missing any genuinely alarming warning flags.

Make some major decisions slowly as well. The Merge will cloud your judgement and make you want to engage in activities that aren't really smart or safe in the long run. In general, don't make mistakes because you're "so in love," because infatuation is a fleeting emotion that will pass.

Stage 2: Doubt and Denial

Doubt and Denial is the second stage of a partnership, where we begin to notice the inconsistencies between ourselves and our partners. With a thump, we awaken from our infatuation coma, only to discover that the characteristics that once appeared so perfect have started to irritate us. (His dependability has become rigid; her kindness has become irresponsible; and their adventurous disposition has become an unwanted risk.)

Unfortunately, as we come up against each other's differences, discord is inevitable. When power dynamics escalate, we are astounded by our partner's transformation. Irritation and loneliness coexist with feelings of affection. Over all, maybe we're not "right" for each other.

Our biological responses to stress increase as our dissatisfaction grows. We may choose to fight or retreat depending on our personality and circumstances. For example, you may feel compelled to struggle to protect your ideals, which may be misinterpreted as a wish to get your way in all. It makes no sense to expect another person to be just like us, but many of us do wonder, "Why aren't you like me?" on some level.

What To Do In This Relationship Stage.

Conflict resolution skills are critical at this stage. Learn how to de-escalate tensions and confront relationship issues head on by treating one another with care and concern. Remember that power conflicts and disagreements are common in relationships; they aren't always indicative of the end of marriage or that the partnership isn't functioning. You'll have to try to distinguish between healthy conflict and unhealthy power issues; the former can be worked on, whilst the latter can indicate that you should end your relationship.

Since now is the period in a partnership where you're beginning to notice the differences, it's also a good time to learn your love languages. There are five love languages, and it's crucial for each partner to understand how they want to be loved.

Stage 3: Disillusionment

The Disillusionment period is the third stage of a relationship. This is love's winter season, which for some couples may feel like the end of the line. The power struggles in the relationship have finally surfaced at this stage, and the problems that the pair has repeatedly brushed under the rug are now glaringly clear. Some people develop a constant state of vigilance, ready to strike at the first sign of trouble. Other couples may slowly drift apart over time, devoting less and less attention to the relationship and focusing more on things outside of it.

Our first taste of romantic love is always a distant memory at this stage. The "I" reappears, a state that feels much more secure than our previous blissful "we" experience. Some partners, however, do not doubt their commitment; rather, they may interpret this as a clear signal that things need to improve.

What To Do In This Relationship Stage.

Make room for yourself by clearing the air. Stop sweeping problems under the rug and ignoring problems; as exhausting as the constant debates can be, sweeping them under the rug just results in a lumpy carpet with a lot of things to fall over.

At this point, there could be a lot of toxic energy in the relationship. To counteract this, make a habit of expressing love even though you're angry. Will you be furious and conscious that something isn't progressing and needs to be discussed whilst still going out to dinner to see a movie together?

During the Merge, the brain just sees the constructive and ignores everything the contradicts that perspective. The brain is focusing on all of the flaws in the relationship at the Disillusionment period. The aspects that are going well are overlooked, while the things that are going wrong receive all of our attention. Attempt to counteract this by cultivating a gratitude practise.

Stage 4: Decision

Since you've reached a breaking point in your relationship, the fourth stage is called the Decision. Self-protective habits, emotional breakdowns, and fleeing the home for hours to get away from each other after a confrontation are all normal. Indifference and distance are also problematic.

When you start seriously considering leaving and even making arrangements to leave the relationship, you know you've arrived. You may be in the mood for a fresh start with a new individual.

At this point, we must choose between leaving, staying and doing nothing about how miserable we are, or staying and working to repair the relationship.

What To Do In This Relationship Stage.

When I see couples at this stage, I often advise them to take a different direction, which is to try to do some work before making a relationship decision. Many partners believe they want out of their partnership, but with the right communication skills, years of frustration or estrangement will melt away.

Doing the work entails recognizing your own part in the breakdown of your relationship and contributing to lasting improvement. If we choose the last option, we will be able to learn lessons that will help us become the best people we can be while still allowing our relationship to develop and deepen.

And if a couple decides to split up, they will usually do so in a positive manner, wishing each other well and acknowledging their own position in the situation.

Stage 5: Wholehearted Love

Wholehearted Love is the fifth stage of a relationship, and it is when our relationship is at the healthiest and most satisfying. Summer is the season of passion, when the fruits of a couple's labors are absolutely ripe and ready to be savoured. Couples undergo genuine individuation, self-discovery, and recognition of imperfection in themselves and their partners, realising that no "perfect match" exists.

This fifth stage of a relationship also requires hard work, but the difference is that partners today know how to listen well and lean into difficult talks without feeling intimidated or threatening one another.

Couples begin to play together again at this stage. They will joke, relax, and have a great time with each other. They can also partake in some of the Merge's exciting passion, joys, and sex as each person rediscovers themselves in ways that allow them to fall in love with each other all over again.

What To Do In This Relationship Stage.

Take care of yourself. The virtues of two wholehearted people power the Wholehearted Love stage: generosity, humour, flexibility, resilience, strong boundaries, self-care, and a meaningful and purposeful life. Couples will remain in this stage as long as they can maintain their own wholeness as people, but make self-care and self-growth targets for the long term.

Recognize that new challenges will loom in the future, so that you will be well-prepared to meet them as they do. Meanwhile, take pleasure in the ride.

WHY WE REALLY NEED RELATIONSHIPS IN LIFE

Relationships are important for a variety of reasons, including improving our mental well-being, building consistency, learning how to be a good friend or partner, finding someone to rely on and trust in times of need, and having someone to talk to when we encounter difficulties. Friends and mates often help us feel less alone and included.

- of our relationships causes us to have different reactions, which make us develop and learn about ourselves. Relationships are also the anchor that keeps people together in tough moments and when we are going through life's challenges. We would have a deadened spirit and a sense of attachment to our true self if we didn't have relationships!

Relationships are necessary for men and women in different ways and for different reasons. Since we share relatable professions, places we visit, social habits and interests, we seem to gravitate toward those that are similar to us. This necessitates the formation of relationships in order to surround ourselves with others who improve us.

Men and women, on the other hand, have different ways of forming lifelong relations with others. Women are much more emotionally invested and dependent on their girlfriends or partners for things like parental guidance, sexual satisfaction, someone to assist with our children's growth and cognitive skills, and learning how to be better at life and in relationships. Men do not need to be physically dependent to derive physical gratification from other women, but they do value closeness almost as much as women do.

When it comes to things like going to the gym or attending athletic matches together, men are not nearly as emotionally involved. In reality, most men turn up, do the action, and then leave without even considering what went wrong, whether there were any misunderstandings, or whether the other party is okay. In relationships, men are better at compartmentalising their feelings, while women prefer to keep grudges, take longer to cope with relational baggage, and let problems fester.

Men progress across marriages more quickly than women, making it possible for them to bond with people of the opposite sex and those of the same sex. Relationships also double as mirrors, revealing areas that we need to improve in order to be better partners and companions. Also, our friends and long-term relationships encourage us to be open and ask for support in ways that we wouldn't usually do with total strangers.

When we're in relationships, we always meet new people from the people we already know and expand our circles! It's exciting to have a diverse range of life experiences, to better understand who people are, to teach them new knowledge, and to embark on new journeys together!

Relationships teach us how to love and be loved, as well as who we want to be and who we don't want to be in life. We will be our true self when we have extreme, trustworthy relationships. We must be open to meeting new people, and spiritual links will assist us in growing our spirituality and inspiring others to open their minds to new possibilities.

Simply be yourself, and the right people will find their way into your life for the right reasons! Always be yourself, and everyone will praise you for it!!

NEWLY IN LOVE? HERE'S WHAT TO KNOW ABOUT STARTING A NEW RELATIONSHIP

Any new friendship is normally a lot of fun at first (albeit a little stressful). Consider this: Someone you adore thinks the same thing about you. Is there anything more than that? Even if both sides are on the same emotional page, it's still important to uphold decorum and, no matter how much you love each other, there are certain ways to start a new relationship that can completely derail it.

Of course, it's normal to feel deep love and desire towards the person you're seeing, but being so enamoured with them can lead you to overlook possible red flags, such as a misalignment of our core beliefs and values.

Follow these simple do's and don'ts to guarantee your dreamy opening scenes transform into a feature-length romance.

Get Your Dates More Diverse

It's a good idea to mix things up early on. Instead of watching Netflix and relaxing, she recommends going on morning walks with friends, setting up lunch dates, and enjoying the company of friends and coworkers. "Watching your mate negotiate diverse scenarios and interactions can be enlightening," she says. Plus, monotony is one of the easiest ways to end a relationship, so strive to stop getting caught in a rut early on by making each date exclusive. Keep in mind that a nice date with your new girlfriend doesn't have to be expensive.

Don't Blow up His Phone

Any date will sound like the first date in a new relationship because there's so much to talk about: where you went to school, what your hometowns are like, and how many pets you had as a child, to name a few things.

If he is used to you doing all of the organising and reaching out, he'll stop bothering because he knows you'll do it anyway.

Spending every waking minute with a new girlfriend will make you lose track of yourself and your mates. "Partners retain a sense of freedom in the longest-lasting marriages," Campbell adds. "See family and friends, keep exercising and working hard, and prioritise alone time; it's vital to strike a balance." When you make your new love the centre of your universe, you put a lot of emphasis on the relationship to be your only source of pleasure and fulfilment.

Don't Skip the Sexual Health Conversation

"It's not yet the time to have sex if you're not happy asking them about STDs and STIs or educating them about your own sexual wellbeing," Dr. Campbell admits. Before getting personal, wait until you're both happy having an open and frank talk about your health. You'll be able to enjoy it more and have more confidence in the relationship as a result.

You should also not be embarrassed to discuss sex outside of the context of fitness. Tell your mate what you do, don't enjoy, and would like to try.

Do Watch Out for Red Flags

According to Campbell, ignoring red flags just delays the relationship's eventual end. "They're obviously not worth engaging in for the long-term," she says, if your new love criticises you, makes plans and then cancels them, you find her lying, or you see him treat people badly. It's tempting to put on rose-colored glasses when you like someone and you want to see the best of them, but it's also important to see the whole person, not just the positive aspects.

Don't Be Close-Minded

Try to keep an open mind when it comes to consuming new diets and engaging in new hobbies. The beginning of a new relationship can be lighthearted though enjoyable, and things will get more serious over time. With that in mind, maybe keep discussions about intensely divisive issues to a bare minimum at first.

Do Respect Yourself

Treating yourself well sets a good precedent for your mate and communicates what you can and will not accept. There's nothing wrong with being principled, self-aware, and authentic. Make time for yourself as well. If he calls and invites you out for an impromptu date, but you need a self-care night to throw on a face mask and snuggle with your furry pet, propose a new date night.

Don't Denigrate Yourself

"Find a way to explore or share these items in a constructive manner if you have things in the history that you deem less than ideal—for example if you either got fired or your previous partner cheated on you," Dr. Campbell suggests. It's never a smart idea to keep this stuff hidden unless you want her to see you in a certain way.

Being insecure is a natural part of dating, particularly in the early stages of a new relationship, so there's no need to feel embarrassed about discussing previous relationships (or anything else, for that matter). No one needs perfection, so it's not important to hide perceptions that have shaped you into the person you are now.

Don't Have Sex Too Soon

We live in a sex-positive age, which means we don't think

you can wait a set period of time before having sex with your new girlfriend for the first time. "Every couple has a different period of time to wait before having sex; there is no such thing as too soon or too long. When all parties are 100 percent, it is the right time ""I'm ready," says Dr. Campbell. In a new relationship, the worst thing you can do is have sex before you're ready and you're afraid he'll lose confidence if you wait.

Do Communicate Often and Well

Be direct and considerate, choose your battles carefully, treat your companion well, and resist negative behaviours such as yelling, insulting, and judging. Since you know your childhood friends too well, you may feel as though you can read their minds, but that kind of closeness takes time, and unfortunately, years together is what you and your new partner lack. You can't trust him to figure out what you're thinking, just be as open and honest as possible.

Already In A Relationship: Here's What To Know About Relationships

Have you ever seen butterflies at the onset of a new love relationship when you don't want to ruin it? You're not alone in your fear of starting a new relationship. "A new partnership is full of promise, opportunities, and exploration," says dating and relationship specialist Andrea Syrtash, "not just of our partners but also of ourselves and our likes, wishes, and desires."

Have the past at the back of your mind.

When dating someone new, often people make the mistake of bringing all of their worries, doubts, and previous bad relationship encounters into their current relationship.

Don't Make Comparisons

It's tempting to start comparing your relationship or your partner to other relationships or partners right away, but it won't help you or make your partner happy.

Look at Actions More Than Words

It makes no difference if anyone is planning vacations for next year if he or she is unavailable right now. You want to make sure you're interpreting acts rather than trusting what the individual says in this situation.

Be Vulnerable, Even if You're Afraid

For certain people, the prospect of being helpless is terrifying. When you're dating someone young, revealing this side will help to strengthen your bond and establish confidence. Vulnerability can be a blessing to someone who wants to get to know you better.

Don't Embellish the Truth or Brag

For both men and women, boasting is a major turn-off. It's not important to try to impress your partner all of the time, particularly if they already like you. You should be proud of who you are even though you don't mention any of your achievements.

Stay in the Moment

Remind yourself that being in a new relationship is an exciting period of exploration and experimentation (and a lot is going to be new all at once). Remind yourself to be present and open to relieve stress. This also applies to being true to yourself and trusting your instincts. It doesn't matter if anyone seems to be fine on paper if they aren't the best fit for you.

Refrain From Being Needy

Jealousy in small amounts can be called cute and safe. Having unreasonable demands on your partner's time and excluding them from doing activities they enjoyed before you began dating is, however, a red flag. According to the expert, it's typical for newly dating couples to spend a lot of their spare time together and giving up some of their normal time with friends and family. However, don't email, call, or claim to see the S.O. all the time because that will stress them out and maybe encourage them to peddle back.

Don't Give up Time With Family or Friends

It's normal for couples in new relationships to forego some of their regular hobbies and break plans with friends in order to spend time with their partner.

Remember the expectation of meeting your partner and creating some space both contribute to attraction.

When you still abandon something to be with your new partner, it can create the impression that your former relationships are less important than who you're dating. When you change your schedule in moderation, keep yourself occupied and respect your plans with friends.

Listen and Stay Curious

Many people struggle with listening as a skill and a communication tool. When you owe your partner your complete attention, they will feel heard and loved. When you express concern in who they are and what they're up to, it not only shows that you care for their lives, but it also makes them feel special.

CHAPTER THREE

Red Flags In A Relationship That Signal It's Time For A Change

It's not until the end of a relationship that we get a good picture of what happened and when things went wrong. Warning signals that we might have overlooked when engrossed in the ecstasy of a new romance or deep into a relationship in which we've spent so much time and effort instantly become glaringly obvious. However, it's important to be on the lookout for red flags in a relationship while we navigate a new romance and get to know another. These warning signs indicate unhealthy habits and patterns that can damage you in the future.

Psychiatrist Abigail Brenner says, "A red flag is a strong intuitive picture to help you process what you're actually experiencing." "People always say at the conclusion of a tough relationship, "He (or she) told me who he (or she) was from the beginning, but I just didn't listen." To stop falling into these traps and spending time with someone who isn't right for you despite the fact that the warning signals have been there all along. We've compiled a list of some of the most common relationship red flags.

Read on to learn how to spot red flags in a relationship.

Lack of Communication

"Can you and your wife articulate yourself while dreaming about your days, your romantic interests, your future hopes, or even your holiday desires?" Jill Weber, a clinical psychologist, poses the question. Take care if your partner shuts down or switches the subject when you bring up emotional content, according to Weber. When a couple is a good pair, both parties find it easy to be honest with one another, even though they don't reveal their darkest secrets at first. You want to hear more about your relationship and share what you've learned.

Lack of Trust

Keep an eye out on someone who has a hard time being honest with you. If dishonesty is a trained coping mechanism rather than planned and malicious, it is also a big red flag. Brenner concludes that "a person who makes himself or herself unaccountable for their conduct lacks honesty and reverence for their spouse."

Your Friends and Family Don't Approve

"If there's something "wrong" about this individual that those who know you well notice, you should pay attention to what they're doing," Brenner suggests. She recognises that we can be defensive when it comes to questions about our new mate when we're in a new relationship. However, there are occasions when an outsider's viewpoint is needed. If you don't have to follow your worried friends and family members' advice, it's worth it to at least listen to what they have to say.

Controlling Behavior

This is a clear red flag whenever the mate tries to "divide and conquer," as Brenner puts it, "driving a rift between you and other important individuals in your life," such as friends and family. Your companion should not be able to dictate where you go, who you meet with, or how you spend your time.

Tip: Your partner can portray this controlling behaviour as an expression of "respect," but understand that it is actually a toxic behaviour.

Wanting Different Things

Although it's fun to have different perspectives and even contrasting views from your partner, Weber warns that for long-term aspirations, you and your partner should have a common vision. She recommends talking about the future with your husband and then considering the major areas where you agree and disagree. Take what they say seriously, and don't believe you can persuade or trick them into doing things they have said they don't like, such as having children, participating in sports, or staying in a certain part of the world. "People are who they are," Weber says, "and these kinds of gaps can become major stumbling blocks to satisfaction over time."

Not Being Able To Be Your True Self

According to Weber, the best part of a long-term relationship is finding someone that knows you inside and out and always likes you. "Notice whether you're putting on a show with your mate, or if you're preoccupied with saying or doing the right thing in their presence," she advises. "Also, see how your companion can relax his or her guard around you." A comfortable ease is needed to form a relationship with your partner that lasts beyond the attraction, and it is this intimacy that allows couples to take risks together.

Abusive Behavior

Abuse is one of the "red flags" that can never be rationalised, excused, or accepted. "Every kind of violence, from the apparently mild to the overtly obvious—verbal, mental, psychological, and definitely physical abuse—is not just a red flag but a giant banner warning you to get out immediately and never look back," Brenner stresses.

FREQUENTLY ASKED QUESTIONS ABOUT LOVE AND RELATIONSHIPS

How Can You Restore A One-Way Relationship?

Talk to your partner about your feelings. Having an open and honest conversation with your partner about how you feel before making arrangements to leave or blowing up in a potential dispute.

Explain whether you believe you're in a one-sided relationship to him or her, and provide advice about how to change the situation.

Is It Normal For Feelings In A Relationship To Fade?

Feelings do not vanish! It's fairly normal in relationships for people to do a lot of things right after starting a relationship; this is good and there must still be an optimistic jiff about everything, but they forget that it's just a part of life, not life itself.

How Do I Know If I've Fallen Out Of Love?

9 scientific signs that you're falling out of love

Their imperfections start to stand out. Yulia Mayorova/Shutterstock.

• Communication reduces

• You develop a wandering eye

• You've fallen for someone else.

• You stop thinking about a future together

• You don't want to be intimate anymore

• Your priorities change

• You feel stucked.

More items

Can You Ever Stop Loving Someone?

You can bring those feelings with you in any manner at all times. Love does not necessarily vanish just because we want it to. And if you can't really quit loving someone who doesn't love you or has hurt you, you can handle your emotions in constructive, safe ways so they don't hurt you further.

Can You Lose Feelings For Someone But Still Love Them?

This is normal early in marriages, and it's usually (though not always) what draws two people together. It is possible to lose this feeling while still loving your mate. You may always love them, but you are no longer in love with them. And it's possible that's the case."

When To Call It Quits On A Relationship?

You keep telling them to make a decision on the next step in your relationship, but they don't know what they want...in life or in your relationship. They might say they can't live without you, but they'll never commit to really living with you.

How Long Does It Take For Love To Fade?

How long do you think such feelings of love will last? "People should expect depressive symptoms for around six months after a divorce and should improve their self-care and social support during this time," Fisher said. As Fisher points out, falling out of love takes time and is entirely normal.

Can Lost Feelings Come Back?

What isn't real is that emotions can't be recovered until they've been destroyed. However, attempting to persuade your ex that he or she is wrong, begging for a second chance, and/or implying that counselling is ineffective are all futile. When your ex says, "I've lost feelings for you," the first thing you can do is figure out why.

Will He Come Back After No Contact?

Yes is the short response. If your ex really has positive feelings for you and you didn't lie, manipulate, or trick him or her, he or she will most likely touch you again after a period of no contact. The outcome, like most things in life, cannot be predicted with 100% certainty.

Can You Love 2 People At The Same Time?

"You can absolutely fall in love with two people at the same time," he says.

You may fall in love with a second person who makes you feel protected, loved, and profoundly connected. Your brain produces dopamine for all of them at the same time and they make you feel special and valued in separate ways."

Does True Love Exist?

True love does exist, but it isn't quite as widespread as many people believe. Love does not necessarily imply compatibility, nor does it imply that people are destined to be together for the rest of their lives. I assume that people should have many true loves in their lives.

Can You Unlove Someone You Love?

It is easy to unlove another, believe it or not! Of course, if it was real love, it would last forever. However, because you've broken up with them, the odds of it being real love are slim to none.

Will No Contact Work If She Lost Feelings?

Since she still feels physically detached and distant, simply avoiding touch will not succeed in the short term. Unfortunately, this is how often, if not many, breakups occur.

Give her some room and back off if you remember she hasn't felt anything in a long time.

Can Love Fade Away And Come Back?

Genuine love is deep, it does not come and go, and it is something that is going to last a long time. This isn't to say that passion doesn't go away; it can, but it leaves certain scars, or potential emotions that can grow if and when the conditions are right.

When Should You Walk Away From A Relationship?

If you wake up one morning and remember you don't know who you are because you've changed too much to make your significant other happy, it's a sure indication you should end the relationship. True romantic love does not necessitate the alteration of another person.

What Are Signs Of Emotional Detachment?

Symptoms of emotional detachment: difficulty forming or maintaining personal relationships. a lack of attention, or appearing preoccupied when around others. difficulty being loving or affectionate with a family member. avoiding people, activities, or places because they're associated with a past trauma or event.

THE CRISES OF THE RELATIONSHIP: RECONCILIATION OR ABANDONMENT

Signs Your Relationship Isn't Working

A partnership has its own set of issues. Also, the best couples will have some difficulties. However, some problems are more akin to gigantic summit than minor stumbling blocks. It's tough to decide whether to hash things out or call it quits when you feel like your relationship has deteriorated.

There are some symptoms that you can't forget, whether you've been having sex or can't seem to stop fighting.

Here are eight signs that your relationship isn't working, as well as what you should do and try to repair it and when it's time to call it quits.

1. You're Always Fighting.

All couples fight. It's natural to fight once in a while, and if handled effectively, it may also be a symbol of a good partnership. When fighting becomes unnecessarily negative, arrogant, and more than you can emotionally handle, it becomes an issue.

According to studies, for every negative interaction, a stable relationship needs at least five positive interactions. Your relationship has become unhealthy if you constantly bring each other down, if your fights turn into shouting matches for the slightest stuff, or if you waste your time tip-toeing between blow-ups.

Is it possible to get your relationship back on track after all of the strife?

What You Can Do

If you and your partner are still arguing, it might be time to get therapy to help you talk about your problems in a safe way. A couple's psychologist serves as an impartial mediator that can assist you in working well together without escalating into a storm over who's "right" or "wrong." Rage control, how to de-escalate an argument, and how to express anger without being contemptuous are all topics covered.

When to Break Up

If the arguments still turn into physical or emotional violence, it's time to end the relationship. You can quit if your mate shoves, beats, or grabs you, or if they gaslight you by saying you're imagining violent behaviour. Even if you've tried therapy and still can't stop debating, it's time to think about stopping it. Any marriages are just too dangerous to save and aren't worth fighting for.

2. There's No Intimacy.

In every relationship, it's perfectly natural for love to wane. Outside stressors such as an exhausting career and young children all have an expected effect on your sex life, and the honeymoon doesn't last forever.

However, there is a distinction to be made between sexual ups and downs and having no attraction for each other. If there is no longer any attraction between you and your mate, or if the idea of touching them makes you uncomfortable, something is seriously wrong.

What You Can Do

Have an open and frank dialogue with your partner; they might be experiencing similar feelings. If you're still overwhelmed with work or home, making a promise to share more physical intimacy together may be beneficial. Set a date in the calendar for next week and adhere to it. You should also want to be more affectionate in your everyday life — a surprise kiss or a playful squeeze can make your companion feel desired and valued.

When to Break Up

It's time to consider leaving the relationship if the lack of sex life has been a persistent source of friction or contempt, or if your wife refuses to address the subject or make any changes. Though sex isn't the most important aspect of a long-term relationship, it is an essential component of feeling linked and loving. You must be frank with yourself on whether you wish to be in a relationship with no physical contact or love.

3. There's No Trust.

You need to be able to count on your companion as you go through the highs and downs of life. Without confidence, you can't have a stable, long-lasting relationship, but how do you create an unbreakable bond, or rebuild one that's already been broken?

What You Can Do

Confidence can be difficult to establish, particularly if you or your partner has betrayed that trust in the past. Some individuals are simply distrustful, and they may be transferring their own insecurities or previous betrayal encounters into the other person. It's best to get therapy in these situations to focus on trust problems.

You should take action within your partnership as well. Aim to earn loyalty over time by upholding small promises — just showing up when you say you'll show up can be a big move.

Real vulnerability can also be practised by showing up to your mate as the most genuine version of yourself. You'll begin to build a connection when you share intimate or negative experiences. When you've done something wrong, be honest about it, and be able to apologise when you've made a mistake. You have to have each other's backs at the end of the day.

When to Break Up

The blunt reality is that if there is no confidence in your relationship, it is unlikely to succeed. Building confidence takes time and commitment, and whether you or your wife refuses to put in the effort, you can break the relationship. It's important to feel secure in your relationship; you deserve to have someone you can depend on.

4. Jealousy Is Getting The Better Of You.

We all have jealous feelings at some point in our lives, but the trick is to control them so they don't become a drag on the relationship.

Although some jealousy is natural, it can easily become toxic if your partner becomes possessive or abusive as a result of it.

The question is, how do you turn things around?

What You Can Do

Since jealousy is normally the result of deep-seated fear, a jealous partner should resolve their own insecurities rather than forcing them into the other party. Consider getting psychological help if you or your partner are having

When to Break Up

It's not cool if the partner's jealousy is out of control and they fail to improve or get treatment. You could end the relationship if they are constantly snooping through your devices, stalking your place, lashing out, or being violent or controlling in some way.

5. You Don't Spend Much Time Together.

One of the most critical aspects of a relationship is spending meaningful time together. This is your one-of-a-kind opportunity to laugh, listen, and engage in constructive dialogue (beyond the standard "How was your day?").

This can be a challenge if you find yourself spending less and less time together or not organising things together.

What You Can Do

Make a commitment to share time together. Choose a night of the week as your date night and don't cancel unless it's an emergency. Some couples avoid boredom by doing something fun and interesting together, such as visiting a new gin bar or taking a weekend trip to a different place. For some, a date night consists of nothing more than snuggling up on the sofa with a movie.

When to Break Up

It's time to move on if you're making arrangements for anyone but your wife and it's obvious you don't like hanging with them any longer.

6. You Have Issues With Change.

Change and growth are inevitable in any relationship, but they can also be a cause of conflict.

Accepting your mate for who they are is, on the one hand, an essential aspect of a romantic relationship. This is a dilemma whether you or your wife are constantly trying to alter or dominate each other.

In the other hand, certain people know they need to make improvements but fail to get support with personal or friendship issues. You can assist your companion in making progress, but how do you decide when to give up if they refuse to consider assistance?

What You Can Do

Avoid pressuring your partner to adjust and accept them for who they are. Allow the little details to slip and just focus on all of the qualities you like about them. If there are more serious concerns, such as personal addiction or family troubles, seek clinical advice from a psychologist.

When to Break Up

It's time to leave if the relationship has become dysfunctional and you or your wife is completely opposed to healthy reform, even after truthful talks and clinical counselling.

7. Your Emotional Needs Aren't Being Met.

When your partner fails to meet your emotional needs, you can experience loneliness or anger, all of which are toxic to any relationship.

It's important that you and your partner are on the same page when it comes to your desires (such as empathy, empathy, and respect), and that you're both able to listen to each other without being disrespectful or aggressive.

What You Can Do

Have an open and honest conversation with your partner. Any relationship requires good communication, and you must be honest about your emotional needs. Before finally rejecting the partnership, give the partner the chance to make improvements. It's also likely that making improvements would require you to look inside yourself.

When to Break Up

There's no need to delay if you've addressed it with your partner and they refuse to alter or want to ignore your questions. Stop the engagement for your own sake.

8. You're Thinking About Cheating, Or You Already Have.

In any relationship, fantasising is natural — but daydreaming on occasion is not the same as repetitive fantasising that starts to damage your relationship.

If your gaze wanders too far, or if you've even had an emotional or sexual affair, your relationship is doomed.

What You Can Do

Make a conscious attempt to return your mind to your girlfriend. Remind yourself why you're with them and what you like about them, and guide your fantasies toward them. If you've ever cheated on your partner, either emotionally or physically, you'll need to have an open and honest talk with them about ending your relationship.

When to Break Up

If you're always fantasising or having affairs, you've actually already mentally checked out of your relationship. When you've already decided you like someone else, it's time to tell your mate and call it quits.

It's important to note that each relationship is unique, and what may be a dealbreaker for one couple might be something that another couple is able to work through.

Aside from physical or verbal abuse (which is grounds for breaking a relationship), all problems can be resolved with time, commitment, and clinical assistance.

Whether you've worked hard and things haven't changed, or if your partner refuses to adapt, or if you're just unhappy. It's time to prioritise yourself and move on.

WAYS TO HANDLE CRISIS IN YOUR RELATIONSHIP

As you first enter a relationship, keep in mind that there will still be ups and downs, particularly after the 'honeymoon' period has passed; this is when you will be able to see it more plainly and be more rational about the relationship. It's not really going to be rosy in a relationship. There will be moments where things aren't that easy in your relationship, no matter how sweet or smooth it is. Most relationships, particularly long ones, go through tough patches because you've been with this person for a long time and the sparks in the relationship have faded. This does not imply that the engagement must end, or that your wife no longer loves you or wishes to leave you for someone else. It is a process that any relationship goes through, and you must take steps to ensure that it does not result in breakup.

Accept It

First and foremost, you must agree that this stage is unavoidable. When you and your partner aren't feeling the friendship and it seems like there isn't any more passion and it's about to end. Face the fact that this is a process that any relationship goes through, and if you divorce your partner because of it, it will happen again in the next relationship. You don't want to be bouncing from one human to the next, but instead of fleeing, try to improve things.

Remember The Beginning

You would go all the way back to the beginning. Mind the little stuff you like about your girlfriend, the honeymoon period, and why you entered the relationship in the first place. Consider that you choose them over all else, and the things they did that touched your heart and made you fall in love with them. How amazing they were, how loving, caring, and romantic they were, how they were the only ones who understood and saw you differently, etc. Consider these things and examine them with those eyes. Examine old photographs and recall how content you were at the start. Remember that the person who was so wonderful is still inside of them; all you have to do is remind them. When you think about these things, you'll remember how insanely in love you two were, and that there's always hope for your future and that you will get through the tough times.

Talk to Each Other

It all begins with communication when a relationship has lost its sparkle. You avoided discussing little details with your partner, such as how your day went, what happened at work, or something amusing that happened on your drive home. The conversations don't have to be intense. Simply converse over dinner or on the phone. Bring back the way you were unintentionally ready to tell your mate of all that happened to you before by being aware of it.

You don't have to see a desire or excuse to speak with them. Call them to see how they're doing, ask about the small stuff, the big things, whatever you want to talk about. And if your companion has avoided telling you anything, the fact that you are communicating as much as possible would encourage them to do so as well. It may be conscious at first, but it will return to being natural over time.

Go On Romantic Dates With Your Partner

Make intimate dates with your partner. Take them to a nice restaurant; it does not seem to have much of an impact on your relationship, but if it is something you haven't done in a long time, it may allow your partner to see life in a new light. Even if you don't have the financial means to do that, you don't have to waste a lot of money on a romantic date with your partner; you should cook, buy some champagne, and do something romantic with them at home. Imagine coming home from work and seeing this surprise nice gesture; it will certainly affect them, particularly because of the timing; things haven't been going well between you two, so the gesture will be appreciated even more.

Spend quality time with your partner outside of dates; take time in your busy work or school schedule to spend a lot of time with your partner. Spending time with your wife will go a long way toward filling the void; you'll see how different things are now, and that will motivate you to make changes.

Be The Change You Are Expecting

Take steps if you're concerned about the state of your relationship. If you desperately want your partner to change, instead of waiting for them to change, try changing yourself. Most marriages die as a result of this. People will wait for their partners to change before they change themselves. You don't have to wait for your partner to take the first step; you can do it yourself and when they hear, they will most likely meet you halfway. It would also demonstrate how serious you are about the relationship.

Don't Lose Hope

This is the most challenging part. It's difficult to keep someone who doesn't understand and support your efforts. Do not lose heart if, after doing all of these things, your partner does not accept them or does not try to improve as well. Give your partner time to change. It may be discouraging because you can feel as though your sacrifices have been in vain, but do not lose hope.

However, if it seems that they are no longer involved in the relationship after a bit, speak to them about it and consider moving on. A friendship is a two-way street, and if the other one no longer wants to be a part of it, you must find a way to let go. You want to be with someone who wishes to be with you, not someone who is controlling you, so come to an agreement and move forward if necessary.

SOLUTIONS THAT CAN SAVE A RELATIONSHIP

It's a rare couple that doesn't hit a few speed bumps in the way. However, once you know what those relationship issues are ahead of time, you'll have a lot better chance of overcoming them.

According to Mitch Temple, marriage and family therapist and author of The Marriage Turnaround, "good partners have learned how to handle the bumps to keep their love life alive" despite the fact that any relationship has its ups and downs. They persevere, solve challenges, and learn how to deal with the complexities of daily life. Many people learn how to do this by reading self-help books and articles, attending seminars, going to therapy, watching other happy spouses, or just trial and error.

1. Relationship Problem: Communication

Problem-solving strategies:

• Schedule a meeting with each other, according to Shimberg. Place your mobile on vibrate, put the kids to bed, and let voicemail take your calls if you live together.

• If you can't "communicate" without yelling, go to a public place like a library, park, or restaurant where you won't be humiliated if someone hears you.

• Create certain ground rules. Try not to interrupt before your companion has finished talking, and refrain from saying something like "You still..." or "You never..."

• Use your body language to demonstrate that you're paying attention. Doodle, look at your watch, or pick at your nails are all bad ideas. Nod to let the other person know you've received the letter, and repeat if necessary. "What I hear you thinking is that you sound like you have more chores at home, even though we're still working," for example.

Whether you're right, the other person will vouch for you. If the other party was just saying, "Oh, you're a slob, and you make more work for me by making me clean up after you," they might phrase it in a better way.

2. Relationship Problem: Sex

Sexually, even couples that love each other may be a mismatch. According to Mary Jo Fay, author of Please Dear, Not Tonight, these issues are exacerbated by a lack of sexual self-awareness and awareness. But, according to Fay, having sex is one of the last things you can give up. "Sex puts us closer together, activates hormones that support our bodies both physically and emotionally, and keeps an intact couple's chemistry healthy," she says.

Problem-solving strategies

• Make a schedule, a plan, a plan. Fay recommends scheduling an appointment, but not late at night because everyone is exhausted. Maybe during the baby's Saturday afternoon nap or a "quickie" before work. Request that friends or relatives take the kids for a sleepover every other Friday night. "Having sex on the calendar heightens the suspense," Fay explains. She also believes that mixing it up a little will make sex more enjoyable. Why not do a little fling in the kitchen? Or do you want to sit by the fire? Or do you want to walk down the hall standing up?

• Allison Cohen, a California psychotherapist, recommends making a personal "Sexy List" to figure out what really turns you and your partner on. Swap the lists and use them to come up with new scenarios that will excite you both.

• If you can't fix your intimate intimacy issues on your own, Fay recommends seeing a trained sex therapist to help you discuss and resolve your issues.

3. Relationship Problem: Money

And before the wedding vows are exchanged, money issues will arise. They can arise as a result of courtship costs or the high cost of a wedding, for example. Couples who are having financial difficulties should take a deep breath and have a meaningful conversation about their finances, according to the National Foundation for Credit Counseling (NFCC).

Problem-solving strategies:

• Be open and frank about the present financial position as a problem-solving strategy. It's impossible to maintain the same lifestyle after things have gone wrong.

• Don't tackle the issue when you're in the middle of a fight. Set aside a period that is both comfortable and non-threatening for both of you instead.

• Accept that one partner can be a saver and the other a spender, realise that both have advantages, and agree to learn about each other's habits.

• Don't conceal your salary or mortgage. To the table, bring accounting records such as a new credit check, pay stubs, bank accounts, insurance plans, loans, and savings.

• Don't blame.

• Construct a joint budget that includes savings.

• Determine who will be in charge of paying the bills on a monthly basis.

• Allow each individual to be self-sufficient by putting money away for them to use as they see fit.

• Develop short- and long-term objectives. Specific ambitions are fine, so you can still have family goals.

• Discuss ways to care for your parents as they age, as well as how to provide for their financial needs if necessary.

4. Relationship Problem: Struggles Over Home Chores

The majority of couples work outside the household, and all of them work several jobs. According to Paulette Kouffman-Sherman, author of Dating From the Inside Out, "it's necessary to equally divide the labour at home."

Problem-solving techniques include being coordinated and straightforward about the roles in the household, according to Kouffman-Sherman. "Make a list of all the positions and decide who can do what." Fairness is essential to avoid frustration.

She advises being open to other options. If you both despise housework, consider hiring a cleaning service. If one of you enjoys housework, the other can help with washing and yard work. You should be inventive to consider your partner's interests as long as it sounds equal to all of you.

5. Relationship Problem: Not Making Your Relationship a Priority

Having your relationship a focal point does not stop until you say "I do" if you want to keep your romantic life alive.

"Relationships begin to lose their allure. As a result, make yours a priority "Karen Sherman, the author of Marriage Magic!, agrees. It's just about finding it, keeping it, and making it last.

Problem-solving strategies:

• Use the same problem-solving techniques you used when you first started dating: Display the gratitude by complimenting one another, keeping in touch during the day, and expressing an interest in one another.

• Make date nights a must. Make time with each other on the calendar, much as every other significant thing of your life.

• Be respectful to one another. Thank you, and thank you, and thank you, and thank you, and thank you, and thank you, and thank you, It communicates to your partner that they are essential.

6. Relationship Problem: Conflict

According to Susan Silverman, a New York-based psychologist, conflict is a normal fact of life. If, on the other hand, you and your wife feel like you're living in your own dystopian version of Groundhog Day, with the same bad scenarios repeating themselves day after day. It's past time for you to break away from your unhealthy routine. You will lessen your indignation and take a cool look at the root problems if you put in the initiative.

Problem-solving techniques:

Problem-solving techniques: Make these tactics a part of your relationship persona.

• Accept that you are not a survivor. It is entirely up to you when and how you respond.

• Be truthful about yourself. Are your words aimed at settling the issue or are you aiming for retaliation while you're in the middle of an argument? It's best to take a deep breath and change your tactic if your words sound accusatory and hurtful.

• Change it up. You can't expect a better outcome this time if you keep responding in the same way that has caused you pain and unhappiness in the past. One small change may have a significant impact. Keep off for a few moments if you normally rush in and protect yourself before your companion has finished speaking. You'll be shocked by how a minor change of tempo will completely change the mood of a conversation.

• Give a little; get a lot. When you make a mistake, apologise. Ok, it's difficult, but give it a shot to see what happens.

"You can't regulate what other people do," Silverman says. "You are the only one in control."

7. Relationship Problem: Trust

A relationship's foundation is trust. Can you see something that makes you doubt your partner? Do you have unanswered problems that make it difficult for you to trust others?

Problem-solving strategies: These tips will help you and your partner build confidence with each other, according to Fay.

• Be consistent.

• Be on time.

• Do what you say you will do.

• Don't lie -- not even little white lies to your partner or to others.

• Be fair, even in an argument.

• Be sensitive to the other's feelings. You can still disagree, but don't discount how your partner is feeling.

• Call when you say you will.

• Call to say you'll be home late.

• Carry your fair share of the workload.

• Don't overreact when things go wrong.

• Never say things you can't take back.

• Don't dig up old wounds.

• Respect your partner's boundaries.

• Don't be jealous.

• Be a good listener.

Even though challenges can still arise in a relationship, Sherman claims that you and your partner should take steps to reduce, if not eliminate, marital problems.

First and foremost, be rational. It's a Hollywood dream to believe that your partner can fulfil all of your expectations and will be able to work them out without you having to think. "Ask for just what you require," she advises.

And, with laughter, learn to let go and love each other more.

Finally, be able to reflect on the relationship and examine what needs to be done. I don't believe it would be any different if someone else was in charge. Until you fix issues, the same lack of qualifications that are causing challenges today will continue to exist and cause issues in the future, regardless of the relationship you're in.

HERE'S WHAT 15 RELATIONSHIP EXPERTS CAN TEACH US ABOUT LOVE

Get Into A Healthy Mindset

1. Look For Someone With Similar Values

Before entering into a marriage, partners should make sure their ideals are compatible.

Other variations can be accommodated and accepted, but a disparity of beliefs is especially troublesome if the target is long-term marriage. Another key to a long marriage is commitment by both parties to make things successful no matter what. Only the couples themselves have the power to split up a relationship." Kelly Campbell

2. Never Take Your Partner For Granted

"This may seem self-evident, but you'd be surprised by how many people seek couples counselling after their partner has decided to terminate the relationship.

It's important to understand that everybody has a breaking point, and whether their desires aren't fulfilled or they don't feel seen by the other, they'll look for it somewhere.

Many people believe that if they are fine without the things they want, their spouse would be as well. The fact that "no relationship is fine" should not be used to justify complacency." Irina Firstein

3. Stop Trying To Be Each Other's "Everything"

"'You are my everything,' is a terrible pop music line and a much worse romantic strategy. No one should be "everything" to all at the same time. Create relationships outside of The Relationship if you want The Relationship to work." Matt Lundquist is a writer who works in the entertainment industry.

Love Is A Verb

4. Do or say something daily to show your appreciation

"Every day, saying and doing brief, basic gestures of gratitude reaps huge benefits. People are happier in relationships when they are accepted as unique and valued, and they are more likely to improve and strengthen those relationships.

And when I say "easy," I'm not joking. Make brief gestures to demonstrate that you're paying attention, such as: Hug, kiss, hold hands, purchase a little present, give a card, prepare a favourite treat, fill the car with petrol, or tell your girlfriend, "You're sexy," "You're the greatest dad," or "Thank you for being so great." Terri Orbuch

5. Make Sure You're Meeting Your Partner's Needs

"The most important thing I've discovered about love is that it's not only an emotion, but a trade and a social interaction. We satisfy our own needs while still meeting the needs of our partners in loving relationships.

Healthy emotions continue to flow as the exchange is mutually satisfying. Whether it isn't, the engagement will die.

That is why it is important to focus on what you and your partner do about each other as acts of affection, rather than on how you feel about each other right now." Jeremy Nicholson is a British actor who has appeared in a number of films, including

Gettin' Jiggy With It

6. Don't Just Go For The Big O

"It's not just about orgasms when it comes to sex." It's all about the sensations, mental affection, stress relief, enhanced fitness (improving the immune and cardiovascular systems), and greater emotional connection with your partner, all thanks to the wonderful hormones released by physical contact. There's more to having sex than just getting off." Kat Van Kirk

7. Don't Forget To Keep Things Hot

"Many times, as time passes, people become more and more shy about the one they love. Couples begin to take their passion for granted, forgetting to stay turned on and seduce their mate.

Maintaining your'sex esteem' on a daily basis is important. This encourages you to keep your love life vibrant, attractive, and engaged." Sari Cooper

8. Remove The Pressure On Performance

"There are stresses associated with the penis-vaginal

paradigm of sex, such as achieving an orgasm at the same time or the notion that an orgasm can occur with penetration. These high expectations put a lot of pressure on people to do well, which leads to feelings of disappointment and dissatisfaction for many people.

Instead, broaden the definition of sex to include something that includes a personal, romantic bond with your partner, such as sensual massages, having a nice shower or bath together, reading an erotic storey together, playing with some fun toys... the list goes on.

And if orgasm occurs, that's fantastic; if it doesn't, that's fine as well. When you broaden the idea of sex and put less emphasis on orgasm and penetration, success anxiety fades and pleasure rises." Holland, Chelsea

It's Not What You Fight For, It's How You Fight " When it comes to conflict, it's not about what you fight about, it's about how you fight.

Contempt, critique, stonewalling (or withdrawal), and defensiveness are the four dispute messages that researchers have discovered will predict whether couples stay together or divorce.

They're called "The Four Horsemen" when they're all together. Rather than using these divisive strategies, battle on a level playing field: Find areas where each partner's target intersects with a mutual common goal and construct from there. Often, emphasise the use of the pronouns "I" and "you." Sean Horan

10. Try A Nicer Approach

Criticism, also known as attacking or accusing one's mate, is one of the relationship's killers.

Begin slowly. 'You always leave your dishes all over the house!' is a better alternative to writing, 'You always leave your dishes all over the place!' Try a more subtle way, relying on your own emotional response and a constructive request.

'When I see dishes in the living room, for example, I get irritated.' When you're done, will you please return them to the kitchen?' Carrie Cole is a singer and songwriter.

11. Identify Your "Good Conflicts"

"Every pair has a 'good conflict,'" says the author. We always find like the thing you desperately desire from your mate is also the thing he or she is least capable of offering you in long-term relationships. This isn't the end of love; rather, it's the start of something much better! Don't flee the situation.

That's where it's going to be. In reality, if you can both call it and commit to working on it together as a couple, it might be the secret to your happiness. Your friendship can become dysfunctional if you treat your 'positive disagreements' with resentment, guilt, or contempt." Ken Page is a writer who lives in California.

Make Time For Self-Care

12. Take Time Apart

"A friend once told me that it's important to take a breather from your relationship, no matter how much you love each other or how long you've been together.

Spend some time with your girlfriends before late at night, go on a weekend trip to see relatives, or just spend some time 'doing you.' You'll all be recharged and able to come back ever more when you return home to Yours Truly." Baglan, Amy

13. Don't Abandon Yourself

"Self-abandonment is one of the most common causes of relationship issues.

We can abandon ourselves in a variety of ways: emotionally (judging or denying our feelings), financially (spending irresponsibly), organizationally (being late or messy), physically (eating poorly, not exercising), relationally (creating tension in a relationship), or spiritually (creating conflict in a relationship) (depending too much on your partner for love).

You will explore how to build a loving bond with your wife as you want to learn to respect yourself rather than choose to abandon yourself." Margaret Paul

14. Create A Fulfilling Life

There's a few. Linda, my wife, showed me that in order for our marriage to succeed, I didn't have to be a hero and risk my own happiness.

She taught me that it was just as important for me to live a fulfilled and happy life for myself as it was for her or the kids.

Over time, it's becoming painfully apparent to me that taking care of myself is almost as vital as taking care of others.

This is better said than done, but it is probably the single most important thing we can do to maintain a mutually fulfilling relationship." Charlie Bloom

The Bottom Line

We might get so caught up in our own expectations that we lose out on the beauty of our relationships and the lessons they teach us. Recognize that no matter how brief a partnership can be, it has meaning.

"A broken romance doesn't exist. Relationships just became what they were supposed to be. It's best not to try to transform a seasonal or transient relationship into a permanent one. Allow yourself to relax and take in the sights." April Beyer

CHAPTER FOUR
Most Common Reasons Couples Break Up

The ten most popular forms of relationship issues that lead to couples breaking up are mentioned below. While not all cause contributes to a divorce, the presence of two or three issues nearly assures the end of a relationship.

Few people enter a relationship wanting it to end badly. Most of us are drawn to a potential partner (often suddenly, sometimes over time), fall in love (slowly or quickly), and plan to commit to a long-term partnership. We do get married on occasion. We're not worrying of or looking for ways to end our relationship.

1. Broken romises, lying, cheating, stealing

This violations of trust nearly often result in relationship issues, which are one of the most common causes for a relationship's failure. When a love relationship's fundamental integrity is constantly undermined, complications arise and desire to stay together dwindles. Couples in loving relationships may learn to work with their disagreements and even endure a physical or emotional affair without being enraged or bitter.

2. A power imbalance, real or perceived

When one partner has more decision-making authority than the other, couples are more likely to split up. When one person makes all of the decisions about hobbies, friends, finances, household affairs, and holidays, the relationship is unbalanced and dysfunctional. All couples should have fair decision-making authority (although in different ways).

3. Acceptance of relationship stereotypes

This used to be a more popular explanation for breakups, but it still persists today! Gender stereotypes contain ideas like "Men should make more money than women" and "Women should stay at home and raise the children." Couples that believe assumptions generate false perceptions, which may lead to breakup.

Husbands, for example, are more likely than wives to choose jobs over families, according to a partnership myth. In fact, either a husband or a wife would prioritise work. It's no longer a matter of gender.

4. Isolation from friends and family

This is a fear-based excuse for breaking up; new partners can distance themselves from others because they're "in love and want to be together." Many partners experience a fleeting period of cocooning, but it is much easier to engage with other individuals on a daily basis.

5. Lack of self-knowledge

It's impossible for one or both spouses to develop a better marriage or stable loving life if they aren't aware of their own wants, wishes, expectations, future aspirations, priorities, beliefs, and tastes. Self-awareness allows couples to express who they are and what they desire in a relationship, which may help to avoid conflicts.

6. Low self-esteem, insecurity, and lack of self-confidence

Couples split up when one person believes the other is incapable of love. This vulnerability will lead to possessiveness and dependency, which isn't good for either partner in a romantic relationship. Insecurity and envy lead couples to split up.

7. Excessive jealousy – one of the most common reasons couples break up

"One of the most common causes of the breakdown of intimate relationships is jealousy," writes Hock. Delusional envy can lead to bullying and aggression, which can (and should) be the reason for a couple's breakup. While delusional jealousy is less prevalent than "natural" jealousy, both can lead to serious relationship issues.

8. Ineffective communication

All couples must be able to communicate their emotions, ideas, beliefs, ideals, desires, frustrations, and joys to one another. Couples who fear speaking freely and hiding their true self do not always end up in a breakup... It does not, however, reinforce their relationship!

9. Control issues

The relationship will become weak or disruptive if one person tries to dominate or exploit the other. Checking in on the partner, calling the partner names, insulting the partner, asking the partner to check in all the time, or not having any exceptions from the routine are all examples of controlling habits.

While these symptoms of obsessive affection do not lead to a breakup, they may indicate an unstable partnership.

10. Unhealthy or abusive physical behavior

Since a surprising amount of men and women remain in unhealthy relationships, it isn't the most common explanation for couples to split up. In a relationship, physical, personal, and emotional violence is difficult. Neither partner may understand why the other treats them the way they do; both partners may wish the relationship to end but are unsure how to do so. It's a complex problem, and it's not the most common excuse for a breakup.

Brutally Honest Phases Of Life After A Breakup

If you've ever been through a terrible divorce, you understand how difficult it can be. Life can be difficult in the weeks (or months, whether it was a really bad one) that follow, but there is still a light at the end of the tunnel. If you have any doubts? Take a glance around. The most of the people you meet have all seen the agony of a divorce at some point in their lives. They made it though and are moving on with their life, so you will as well. And once you get through these painfully frank stages in life following a divorce, you'll not just feel happier, but you'll still be healthier.

That all sounds amazing, but it's not so encouraging because you're sitting in the midst of your heartbreak. However, knowing what to expect will help you figure out where you are in the grieving process and when you'll be able to move forward. Although and the post-relationship journey is unique and unfolds on its own timetable, there are certain shared threads that we all follow, so you don't have to go through this alone. Here are the stages that almost everyone goes through after a divorce.

1. The Black Hole Phase

This is a difficult time. It happens right after the breakup, where it is bleak and hopeless. This is the "stay on the couch and cram foodstuffs into your foodstuffs hole while watching Netflix" period. There will be a lot of moaning and fantasizing about spending the rest of your life single, surrounded by animals.

All you'll miss about your ex, as well as all that makes them the devil incarnate, is all you can think about. It's a difficult time. Although the black hole's agony will sound as though it will swallow you up, it will not. Only be patient with yourself and give it time. It's normal to be sad.

2. The "Friendtervention" Phase

Your mates would eventually tyre of this dark pit process and intervene — not just because they can't bear seeing you injured, but just because they've always felt your ex wasn't good enough for you, and it's time you realised it. They'll drag you off the couch and reacquaint you with your long-lost companions: soap and clean clothing. It's time to get some vitamin D and see the sun again.

Although a part of you wishes to return home to reunite with your couch while watching your Crazy Ex-Girlfriend marathon (you didn't like it the first time you wanted to watch it, but now you know it's freaking genius), another part of you is thankful to your friends for keeping you out of the house.

3. The Boredom Phase

When the dark cloud disappears, you know that you can, in fact, make it through this. You won't be broken by this divorce. You're still tired, but you're up and about and ready to get back into the swing of things. But you're still very bored. The days seem to drag on forever! What was the source of all these extra hours? You tend to understand how much time is consumed just by being in a relationship. Being single is full of possibilities and independence, but if you're new to it, you might find it's dull! So you've decided to participate...

4. The New Routine Phase

After all, you can't just lay around lonely all day, can you? So now is the time to do something you've never had time to do before and create a new schedule for yourself! Filling our time is something that humans are usually excellent at. Your new routine has quickly taken over your schedule, and you're back to being depressed about never getting enough time to rest. So, I think that's So, I think that's improvement.

5. The Lingering Mourning And Relapse Phase

You've begun to feel a lot happier as a result of being busy. Being positive pays off! So maybe now is the time to be serious about bringing the relationship to a close. It's time to delete your ex's social media accounts and return all of their belongings. You're progressing and advancing! What began as a purge turned into a vortex, and instead of just blocking them, you went deep into their Instagram and followed their tags into deeper and darker waters.

Suddenly, you hear the sofa's siren tune, beckoning you to another happy scream. Allow yourself to enjoy it. Relapse is an inevitable part of recovery. However, the next time, simply hit block to keep it moving.

6. The Moving Phase

Those emotional relapses eventually become shorter, less severe, and, most importantly, less frequent. In their position is a sense of acceptance (and even excitement) about getting back out there and seeing what possibilities await. It's actually happening, and that's the message you've been looking for. You've officially healed, and you're more strong than you ever imagined. You've made it to the end of the breakup tunnel, so congratulation!

Remember, it's easy to lose faith after a bad breakup, particularly when it seems like love has died for good, but all it takes is time and ice cream.

WANT TO GET BACK IN THE GAME? HERE ARE 4 EXPERT TIPS FOR DATING AFTER A DIVORCE

Dating is difficult no matter where you are in life. It was overwhelming in high school, complicated in college, and even more complicated as an adult, particularly if you'd never been married before. If you're a 30-year-old woman navigating dating following a divorce, finding someone new will present a whole new set of problems.

"People can stigmatize someone in their 30s who is already divorced and the average age for first-time marriage in the United States is 27 for women and 29 for men," says psychologist Kelly Campbell. "This shame may lead a person to wonder if there is anything wrong with them for divorcing at such a young age, and their self-esteem may suffer as a result."

What is our recommendation? Don't give up and try not to take any dating setbacks too seriously. Whatever the case, dating is difficult, but as long as you remain hopeful and optimistic, you can meet someone with whom you can communicate. Seeking love after a divorce may be difficult, but it's not impossible, according to Campbell. We asked her to explain the attitude and approach that someone in this case should take if they're willing to resume dating, and her advice should help make a difficult situation sound more manageable.

Get in the Right Mindset

People who have been divorced should make an effort to ensure that the problems they had in their former relationship do not change their view on future relationships. When people choose to hide or bury their feelings, they fear having those problems affect them and their relationships in the future. It's difficult to press on because you haven't completely processed your marriage's emotional wounds. Make sure you're happy to date before you download a dating app or ask your friends to match you up with someone.

If you're not sure if you're going on a date with anyone because it's time or because you're curious about the possibility of meeting someone, consider the following queries. One of the most important questions is whether the prospect of opening up to someone unfamiliar excites or frightens you.

Address Your Previous Marriage

When it comes to discussing their former marriage, people should do so without feeling embarrassed. They are who they are because of their divorce, and if a potential mate can't understand it, they aren't a successful match. However, you do not feel compelled to reveal any aspect of your and your ex's breakup. The safest course of action is to inform your future new relationship as soon as possible. We believe that the longer you wait, the more this knowledge will weigh on you, and you will begin to feel as though you are hiding something, which will place a lot of pressure on you.

Keep an Open Mind

Allow yourself to do new stuff, and don't limit yourself to one kind of sexual partner just because that's what you've previously pursued. Consider this: If you marry someone that exactly matched your "kind," you will have to accept that that kind of person isn't right for you so you ended up divorcing.

You don't have to push yourself to go out with someone you know you won't get along with, but you should step out of your comfort zone at least once. You could find someone you never expected to be so satisfied with.

Prioritize Yourself

This is by far the most important thing people can do when they start dating again. It also makes sense. And if you had a good sense of self during your marriage, you most likely only saw yourself as part of a couple. For example, you would not have went on a trip without your partner if you were married. However, now that you're no longer dating, go back to doing things that make you comfortable before re-identifying as a couple.

HOW TO MEND A BROKEN HEART AFTER A HEART-BREAKING GOODBYE

Break up with the person you were once loyal to and desperately in love with, and say your goodbyes. We've both been there, and we understand how it feels.

We've just had our hearts shattered. When it happens to you, it's devastating, because while others can understand, they aren't there. The pain is real and there for you. You can feel utterly powerless at times, as though you'll never be able to overcome your pain.

The key points to note are that there are people who care for you, that there is still a light at the end of the tunnel, and that there are people who can assist you in getting there. You must remember that getting over a breakup can be impossible, but it is just a matter of time.

Here are a few suggestions to help you get back on the path to peace and prosperity.

Cut All The Contact.

Maybe the two of you agreed to remain friends. A post-breakup relationship can develop over time, but the main term here is "time." Few ex-partners make a smooth transition into friendship right away (and if you believe you have, wait before one of you begins dating someone new).

"If the other party caused the split, delete their number from your phone so you don't feel compelled to call them," Lester advises. It will help you stop the infamous drunk-dial and the urge to send inappropriate messages.

This is, without a doubt, the most important rule in a breakup. Maintain a safe distance by not texting, emailing, meeting in person, or calling. When you're at it, delete them from Facebook and all other social media accounts. This doesn't have to be lasting, so it's best not to have their voice in your head when you're vulnerable to hurtful or, on the other hand, caring terms. Moving back into a relationship that isn't working carries a high risk. You could even end up in a verbal brawl, creating even more pain and fear. When it's over, cutting the links for good sets you on a smoother road to recovery.

• Create a "Emergency Contact List" of all of your BFFs' phone numbers so that anytime you're tempted to call your ex to beg for a reconciliation, you can call to speak to your friends instead.

• Choose a hobby to replace your need to email, phone, or stalk your ex, something quick and easy like watching your favourite Netflix show or walking around your favourite local stores.

Let Your Emotions Out.

Cry, weep, shout, and shout your heart out. Find ways to release and let go of whatever suffering you're experiencing as long as it doesn't harm you or anybody else. When people remind you that all breakups are difficult, it's because they are. If you push this part of the healing process away from yourself, it will fester and expand. Regardless of how convenient or difficult the breakup was, you would undoubtedly experience certain negative feelings. Respect your emotions and remember that the more you express them, the less powerful they can get. It assists you in getting past them!

• Listen to depressing music. According to studies, listening to sad music will potentially make us happy. Sad music can help to control depressive emotions and moods, as well as provide relief. If you need a good sob, we've put together a playlist of sad songs for you to listen to. Find a peaceful spot where you can get your thoughts out and relax.

Accept the fact that it's over, at least for now.

Coping with the conclusion of a partnership resembles a 12-step programme in several ways. Staying away from that person would help you understand yourself even faster. This technique is more dependent on time than anything else, but there are ways to speed it up. And if you didn't commit to the divorce, try to look at the case positively. Don't obsess about what should have gone differently. There are an endless number of should-haves and could-haves, and contemplating them will send you spiralling.

Your decisions were important during the time you were in the relationship. They no longer do. Now it's up to you to get to a point where you're not fighting with yourself over how things are. Don't berate yourself and do so with kindness. It can take some time for the heart to catch up with reason, but agree that the friendship is over in the meantime.

• Tell yourself that it's done and that it's time to move on to the next chapter in your life.

• Clean up all that would remind you of your time with your ex. • Talk to your family and friends because it can be difficult to see the bigger picture when you are caught in a situation.

Find Yourself

It's likely that you gave up a bit of yourself in the relationship. This is your chance to discover yourself again, and it can be enjoyable. This is one of the benefits of the breakup, so take advantage of it! Perhaps you gave up a once-loved hobby or started taking scented baths. If you want to eat salad and granola bars for dinner, go ahead. There are many personal aspects that make you unique; all you have to do now is rediscover them and reclaim the feeling. Alternatively, you may have matured in your relationship, allowing you to learn new things about yourself.

• Have an in-depth exploration of your inner-self by having a mindful conversation with yourself.

Asking self-reflective questions will help you learn more about yourself and your true desires.

You may ask the following questions:

1. Can I really do what I'm doing now if "love myself more" is my highest priority in life?

2. What do I like the most about myself?

3. What was my life like before we started dating?

4. What do I want to accomplish in my life and where do I begin?

5. What is the most critical area on which I need to improve?

The path to discover yourself is difficult and most of us don't have time to slow down and consider what we really want. It may be a long trip, but you can take your time and it will be well worth it!

Explore and Have Fun

Bring your girlfriends together and head out when you're about to have some real fun again. Go shopping, partying, or doing a roller coaster. Do something that makes you happy, makes you laugh, and makes you feel good on the inside. Be silly and spontaneous. Take pleasure in your life.

• Do something fresh and fun on your own that you've always wanted to do • Spend meaningful time with friends and family

• Explore and build new patterns (learning a new language is a successful option!) • Reconnect with long-lost friends

Pay Attention to Your Thoughts

Don't reject or cling to your ex's memories while you want to get on with your life. They can resurface in your mind as a reminder of a happier moment (or not). Acknowledge it, smile or cry. Instead of sticking to the past, let it go. Don't look at photos or old messages you received from him on purpose. It's now all about you and the current circumstances. Your ex is a part of who you are now, and you should be thankful for that, but your relationship with them is over.

• As previously said, get rid of something that triggers memories.

• Don't want to get away from your emotions. Face them. To help you declutter your mind, write down how you're feeling. The more you compose, the more you'll be able to pinpoint what causes your emotions and help plan for them.

Understand the beauty of being single and don't rush into another relationship.

Don't rush into another relationship under the impression that you're fine. It's definitely the most convenient solution, but you'll never really forget about your ex. In the long term, you haven't really moved on from your ex, because when your next relationship ends, you'll have two ex-partners to contend with. You're just extending the unavoidable suffering.

• Consider the kind of partnership you want. Understanding your needs when starting a relationship is important and it will help you avoid another heartbreak.

• When you're ready, go out and meet new people. Make sure you speak with them and take your time getting to know them before jumping into a new relationship.

Develop a mindful life.

It's beneficial to cultivate a mindful lifestyle over time so that your mind can remain relaxed and balanced no matter what life throws at you. Being conscientious involves paying attention to yourself and acknowledging your needs, as well as understanding what makes you happy.

Protect your heart with a social media purge.

Facebook and Instagram can be absolute poison for the brokenhearted, whether you're browsing through old images of happy days or refreshing your ex's page to dissect every post.

Trying to figure out if your ex is pleased because he or she shared a brunch photo would just make you feel bad for yourself.

It's not unkind to unfollow an ego-wounded ex, and it's also not unkind to block them in the interests of mental health. By clicking on the three dots in the right-hand corner of a status update, you can opt to "snooze" a Facebook contact for 30 days, which means they won't show in your feed for a month (you'll also need willpower to stop reading their profile).

Schedule plans with friends.

You're still not going to feel fine in the days of a breakup, so try to keep yourself occupied as much as possible. Make arrangements for your mates so you don't waste time moping."

Make a dinner date with your closest friend, and all the more if it turns into an hours-long hangout. If you're the one to put non-romantic relationships on the back burner while you're in love, bring an apology (and the intention to never do that again). You may also focus your efforts on forming new friendships.

Until you send out those invitations, keep in mind that you can just host friends who make you feel like the strongest version of yourself, not those that don't. Right now, your spirit is like a wounded baby animal who wants to be pampered!

Return to the things you love doing, but they didn't.

Remember how you used to love Indian food but your ex would never let you order takeout? Tonight, order curry and try to enjoy the delicious taste of freedom.

When we meet someone new and begin spending a lot of time with them, it's easy to lose track of any of our favourite hobbies. Now that your relationship is over, it's time to get back into regular yoga, biking, or board games, or whatever it was that made you happy that you put on the back burner when you were together.

Travel and explore new places.

Explore a different place to get into a new mindset. It also doesn't have to be an extravagant, Eat, Pray, Love-style solo trip: Start by taking a different route home or going to a restaurant you've never been to before.

It's possible to get trapped in a relationship by going to the same places and doing the same things. Push yourself to visit areas of the city you've never been before, or go on a solo weekend trip to places you've wanted to go but haven't had the opportunity.

Refrain from obsessing and ranting about what went wrong.

We learn a lot about ourselves through our marriages, both positive and bad. Running in circles and getting resentful won't help you learn about yourself and what you want in a relationship. It would keep you enslaved to the troubles of the past.

Agree that the partnership ended for a reason, and now concentrate on imagining what you'd like to give and receive from your next mate. Meditation and counselling are two effective ways to let go of frustration for how you were wronged and avoid taking the subject up again in the future.

CONCLUSION

Thanks for reading till the end of this book. When looking for love, there are many easy things to consider. Is that person sincere when they say "I love you" to you? Can that person make you miss them when you're with them and when you're not with them? Would you do something for that guy, including giving up your own life to defend theirs? In a nutshell, love is the best thing a person can do, and everybody can have it. Some people fall in love too late, and others fall in love at the right time. Some people may believe they have found love, only to come to a halt. The main thing to note is that no one is flawless, and some are less perfect than some, but no matter what happens, you still love that person. Nothing, as previously said, will sever the unique bond that you have with another person if there is genuinely a link between you and that other person. It has the ability to make you do dumb and sometimes insane stuff. Finally, everybody would love to have anyone call them after a long day at work to say, "I love you," or to visit them at home to say, "I missed you, how was your day?" The feeling of being desired is the best gift a person can get, and most people would give anything to have that feeling. As long as love remains between you and the other person, the moments you spend with them will make you smile on the inside and will never be missed. Everyone is waiting for the special someone to love, even though most people say that they will never be able to love. The person is always searching for the piece of themselves, and they will do so until they find it or die. Those who are lucky enough to have seen it and to genuinely feel something about another human while they are with them, thinking about them, or talking to them are the ones who have the missing piece that so many want. If it was love at first sight or a love that grew into something wonderful over time, a piece of their heart has been filled with the other's love.